W9-AYX-794

3367600400359O

DISCARDED

DATE DUE

DEMCO 128-5046

Pablo Picasso

Andrew Langley

Raintree

LA JOLLA COUNTRY DAY SCHOOL
LIBRARY
9490 GENESEE AVENUE
LA JOLLA, CA 92037

Copyright © 2003 Raintree

All rights reserved. No part of this book may be reproduced or utilized in any form or
by any means, electronic or mechanical, including photocopying, recording, or by any information storage
and retrieval system, without permission in writing from the Publisher. Inquiries should be addressed to:
Copyright Permissions, Raintree,
100 N. La Salle, Suite 1200
Chicago, IL 60602.

Published by Raintree, a division of Reed Elsevier, Inc.

Project Editors: Marta Segal Block, Helena Attlee
Production Manager: Brian Suderski
Designed by Ian Winton

Planned and produced by Discovery Books

Library of Congress Cataloging-in-Publication Data:

Langley, Andrew.
Pablo Picasso / Andrew Langley.
v. cm. -- (Raintree biographies)
Includes bibliographical references and index.
Contents: War paint -- Child prodigy -- To Paris -- The Blue Period --
Brighter times -- Going his own way -- In the theater -- Breaking out --
New directions -- The coming of war -- Picasso's palace -- At work till
the end -- A lasting memory.
ISBN 0-7398-6865-9 (HC), 1-4109-0071-1 (Pbk.)
1. Picasso, Pablo, 1881-1973--Juvenile literature. 2.
Artists--France--Biography--Juvenile literature. [1. Picasso, Pablo,
1881-1973. 2. Artists.] I. Title. II. Series.
N6853.P5L26 2003
709'.2--dc21

2002155030

Printed and bound in the United States
1 2 3 4 5 6 7 8 9 0 08 07 06 05 04 03

Acknowledgments
The publishers would like to thank the following for permission to reproduce their pictures:
The Bridgeman Art Library: 4, 6, 7, 9, 10, 12, 13, 14, 17, 18, 19, 20, 21, 22, 24, 25, 26, 27;
Corbis: 8, 11, 15, 16, 23, 28, 29; The Hulton Archive: cover; Peter Newark's Pictures: 5.

Some words are shown in bold, **like this**.
You can find out what they mean by looking in the glossary.

CONTENTS

WAR PAINT

In April 1937 bombers attacked the Spanish village of Guernica. More than 1,600 people were killed in three hours. The aircraft were German, but they had been sent by General Franco, the **Nationalist** leader in Spain's **Civil War**.

The news of this cold-blooded attack reached the Spanish artist Pablo Picasso in his **studio** in Paris. Immediately, he started work on a **gigantic** painting to express his anger. Using only black, gray, and white, Pablo Picasso showed the agony of the victims— fathers, mothers, and children—along with a bull and a screaming horse. Within five weeks it was finished and then shown to the public.

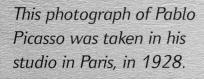

This photograph of Pablo Picasso was taken in his studio in Paris, in 1928.

4

THE SPANISH CIVIL WAR

In 1936 Spain was in the middle of a civil war. General Francisco Franco wanted to have a king instead of a government that people vote for. He also wanted the Catholic Church to have more power than other religions. Franco was helped by Germany's Adolf Hitler. In 1939 Franco took control of Spain, and he stayed in charge until his death in 1975.

Picasso gave his painting the title *Guernica*. In it he showed how horrible war is. He also showed the fear shared by most people at that time. They were right in fearing that a second world war was about to break out.

After the showing in Paris, Picasso's **canvas** was shown in Norway, Britain, and then New York. It remains one of the most powerful pictures ever painted.

Picasso's Guernica *is one of the most famous paintings of the twentieth century.*

CHILD PRODIGY

Pablo Picasso was born on October 25, 1881, in Malaga in southern Spain. His father was a painter, though not a very successful one, and made his living as a drawing teacher. Even as a baby Pablo was thrilled by the pencils and the pictures that he saw about the house. He learned to draw before he could walk or speak.

The Girl with Bare Feet *was painted by Picasso in 1895, when he was only 14 years old.*

In 1891 the family moved to the north of Spain, where Picasso's father had taken a teaching job. Here, young Pablo found ordinary schoolwork dull and difficult. He was far happier in the nearby art college, where he quickly learned new drawing skills.

The Picasso family moved again in 1895, this time to the lively and colorful city of Barcelona. Picasso was only 14 but clearly had such a special talent that he was accepted as a student at the Academy of Arts. Within a year he had his own **studio**. Within three years he had become one of the leaders of Barcelona's artistic community.

*Picasso completed this **portrait** of himself at age 15.*

Passing the Test

To his teachers and friends, Picasso was obviously a genius. What proved this was the speed and confidence of his work, even as a young boy. The entrance exam for the Barcelona Academy was made up of a series of tasks that students were given a month to finish. Picasso completed them in a single day!

TO PARIS

Picasso held his very first show in a scruffy Barcelona café in 1900. But by now he was eager to find new places, new influences for his work, and new experiences. That fall he and a friend, Carlos Casamegas, set out northward for Paris.

This first visit to the French capital was a short one for Picasso, because he soon ran out of money and had to return home. Even so, he fell in love with Paris. He was inspired by the **galleries** with their collections of great paintings, and by the new, adventurous ideas about art that filled the air.

Picasso loved the bustling, crowded, outdoor cafés of Paris.

POETS AND PAINTERS

Paris was an exciting place for an artist in 1900. It had become a center for some of the greatest painters, **sculptors**, novelists, and poets of the time, who enjoyed the feeling of freedom they found there. Among them were the painters Monet, Gauguin, and Cézanne, the sculptor Rodin, and the poet Apollinaire.

The sculptor Auguste Rodin was one of the leading artists in Paris when Picasso first visited.

Picasso returned the following year, and rented a small room in the Montmartre district of Paris where he could live and paint. He worked very hard, producing many pictures that showed the lively cafés and nightlife of the area. At the same time he grew to understand how modern art was heading in fresh and surprising directions.

THE BLUE PERIOD

Soon after Picasso returned to Paris, tragedy struck. His friend Casamegas killed himself. The death added to Picasso's mood of sadness, which he explored in the paintings of what has been called his "Blue Period."

He became obsessed with the color blue, which has always been associated with misery and sadness. Blue is also a cold color, which can add mystery to a painting. Picasso studied the poor people he saw in the streets of Paris and Barcelona. His Blue Period pictures show blind men, a Jewish outcast, beggars, and unhappy mothers with their children.

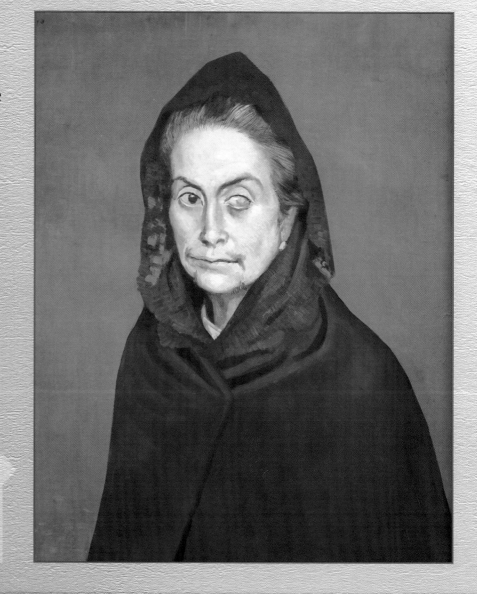

This picture, from Picasso's Blue Period, is a portrait of a woman named Carlotta Valdivia.

The Nimble Rabbit

Picasso and his friends could only afford to eat in the very cheapest cafés. Their favorite was called the *Lapin Agile* ("the Nimble Rabbit"). The owner was very fond of the young artists among his customers, and he sometimes took their paintings as payment instead of money.

The walls of the Lapin Agile *café were decorated with paintings by the customers.*

Picasso was poor as well. He worked very hard, but found it difficult to sell any paintings. In the winter of 1903 he was so poor that he could not afford the rent of his room. He moved in with a friend, the poet Max Jacob. There was only one bed, so Picasso worked at night while Jacob slept. Picasso then slept all day while Jacob worked.

BRIGHTER TIMES

After years of moving back and forth between Spain and France, Picasso finally settled in Paris in 1904. His new home was a dirty, run-down building, again in the Montmartre district, but it was full of noisy and cheerful neighbors. Picasso enjoyed staying in such a lively place.

He was made even happier by meeting the beautiful Fernande Olivier, who was the first great love of his life. This happiness was marked by a change in Picasso's style of painting. He turned away from blues, and began using gentler pink, orange, and gray colors. He also painted new subjects—often circus performers such as acrobats or clowns. This is known as his "Rose Period."

A family of circus comedians, pictured by Picasso in 1905

Picasso stands proudly amid the clutter of his Paris studio.

At last, Picasso was also beginning to make money. He refused to take his work to **dealers** to sell, but adventurous art collectors visited his **studio** to buy his paintings. With these earnings, Picasso and Fernande went on holiday to the Pyrenees mountains, on the frontier between Spain and France.

Picasso's Studio

Picasso liked to work in a cluttered and messy studio. One visitor was amazed at the muddle he found—a broken sofa, torn wallpaper, stacks of pictures covered in dust, white mice, and a huge dog called Fricka. And of course, there was the litter of artist's materials— paint pots, **paraffin**, rags, and brushes.

13

GOING HIS OWN WAY

Picasso was always looking for new ideas and fresh influences. On vacation in the Pyrenees, he began to paint much simpler shapes. In 1906 he studied ancient stone **sculptures**. He was also excited by a collection of carved African masks that he saw in a Paris museum.

All of these things encouraged Picasso to develop a different and exciting style of art. After a long period of preparation, he completed a large painting called *Les Demoiselles d'Avignon* (*The Women of Avignon*) in 1907. It showed a group of nude women, their bodies a collection of sharp angles and their faces like the African masks.

Picasso saw carved masks like this one in the Musée de l'homme in Paris.

CUBISM

Picasso developed the idea of Cubism with another artist, Georges Braque. They did not try to paint pictures that looked like real life. Instead, they portrayed their subjects using a mixture of **geometric** shapes—including cubes. They also showed the subjects from many different points of view at the same time. Cubism changed the way painters saw the world.

The jagged shapes of cubes and pyramids can be seen in Picasso's painting Violin.

His friends were horrified. The picture was not at all lifelike and seemed ugly and brutal to them. Some thought he had gone crazy. Bravely, Picasso carried on painting in his shocking new way. Slowly, people began to understand what he was doing. The unusual style became known as "Cubism."

The Power to Shock

"The picture [Les Demoiselles d'Avignon] *seemed to everyone something mad or monstrous. Braque declared that it made him feel as if someone were drinking gasoline and spitting fire…"*

Daniel-Henry Kahnweiler, an art dealer

IN THE THEATER

Picasso now lived more comfortably, thanks to the sale of his pictures. He had a new **studio**, and a new girlfriend, Marcelle Humbert (Picasso called her "Eva"). He continued to try out bold Cubist ideas—and use new methods. Inspired by Georges Braque, he began to glue paper, rope, and other objects to his paintings.

This happy period of his life came to an end in 1914. World War I broke out, and Paris grew empty as many of his friends went off to fight. The next year Eva died tragically, and the heartbroken Picasso was alone once again.

Picasso designed sets and costumes for the Ballets Russes. This is Alexandra Daniloza, one of the company's leading dancers, in "Swan Lake."

THE NEW DANCE

The Ballets Russes (Russian Ballet) was a company with new and exciting ideas. It used modern music, by composers like Stravinsky, modern set designs, and startling dancers such as Nijinsky. Together, these elements created a different kind of ballet. From now on, Picasso often worked in the theater, which gave him wonderful new opportunities.

The war dragged on, and he tried to work. Then, in 1917 a new world opened up for him. He was invited to go to Rome and design scenery and costumes for the Ballets Russes, a Russian dance company. He was dazzled by the beauty of Rome and the excitement of the theater. He also fell in love again — with Olga Koklova, a young ballet dancer.

*Picasso's **portrait** of Olga Koklova, his first wife*

BREAKING OUT

Picasso and Olga were married in 1918. The couple lived in a large apartment in a wealthy area of Paris, where their son Paulo was born in 1921. By now Picasso was rich enough to dress well and give large parties. He also began to spend each summer by the ocean.

During this period, Picasso moved away from his Cubist style and painted a series of more realistic pictures. Several were gentle **portraits** of his new wife, and others showed little Paulo dressed as a clown or a bullfighter. Many people were disappointed at what seemed like old-fashioned work.

Picasso painted many pictures of his little son Paulo dressed as a **harlequin**.

Then suddenly, in 1925 Picasso shocked everyone with a big new painting called *The Three Dancers*. It was wild and brightly colored, with three **distorted** figures dancing madly. Some friends saw the picture as a sign that Picasso was unhappy in his marriage.

Picasso was fascinated by the shapes of musical instruments. He made this guitar from painted metal.

Do Not Touch

Picasso's violent feelings at this time can be seen in *Guitar* of 1926. This was not a painting, but a **construction**, using an old floor cloth, pasted paper, and string. Picasso hammered nails through the back, and even thought of gluing razor blades on to the frame so that no one could pick it up!

NEW DIRECTIONS

The late 1920s saw many changes in Picasso's world. Even though he was still married to Olga, he began to date Marie-Thérèse Walter. He also started to work on an entirely new project. This was a series of over 100 **engravings** that would take him 10 years to complete. They are now known as *The Vollard Suite*.

PICASSO AND THE BULLFIGHT

Since he was a child, Picasso had loved to watch bullfights. He felt the same about bullfights as he did about life, finding them both scary and beautiful. Many of his pictures show bullfights, bulls, and wounded horses.

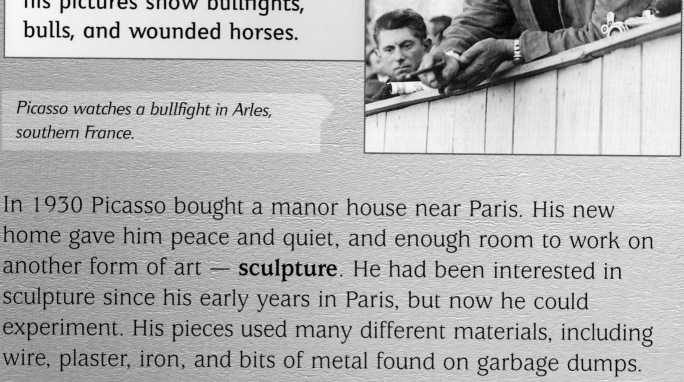

Picasso watches a bullfight in Arles, southern France.

In 1930 Picasso bought a manor house near Paris. His new home gave him peace and quiet, and enough room to work on another form of art — **sculpture**. He had been interested in sculpture since his early years in Paris, but now he could experiment. His pieces used many different materials, including wire, plaster, iron, and bits of metal found on garbage dumps.

At this time, a new figure began to appear in Picasso's paintings and drawings. This was the Minotaur, a character from Greek **mythology** with a man's body and a bull's head. It was a frightening creature, with huge strength and power. Some think that Picasso saw himself as a kind of Minotaur.

The threatening and powerful figure of a Minotaur carries a dead horse.

THE COMING OF WAR

By mid-1935 Picasso was in the middle of what he called "the worst time of my life." He was having trouble with his marriage and personal life. For nine months he could not paint anything. So he shut himself in his manor house and tried another of his talents, writing poetry.

Then in 1936 came the outbreak of the Spanish **Civil War**. This inspired Picasso, who was against Franco. He produced several works protesting Franco's cruel **dictatorship** in Spain, the most famous of them being *Guernica* in 1937.

*A **study** for* Guernica, *showing a woman crying.*

Making Sense

"Everyone wants to understand painting. Why not try to understand the songs of birds? Why can people love a night, a flower, all that surrounds humankind, without seeking to understand it? Yet with painting, people want to understand."

From a magazine essay by Picasso, 1935

By now the threat of war hung over all of Europe. Picasso's paintings showed how scared he was of the new governments in Germany and Italy. These governments did not treat people fairly. They did not allow people to talk freely, and sometimes they tried to control what sort of art people could make. When the Germans invaded France in 1940, Picasso went on working in his Paris **studio**.

German soldiers on the streets of Paris during World War II.

Picasso's Palace

World War II ended in 1945, and France was free again. Picasso left Paris and went to live in Antibes, in the south of France with his new girlfriend, Françoise Gilot. He was given a huge building called the Grimaldi Palace to work in. The pair found a home in a nearby village, and here two more children were born— Claude, a son, and a daughter named Paloma, which means dove.

Picasso with Françoise Gilot and their son Claude in the early 1950s

The hard years of the war had made Picasso more interested in politics. He joined the **Communist Party** and designed a poster for a 1949 youth conference in Paris. His simple picture of a dove became a symbol for the peace movement throughout Europe.

*Picasso with some of his pottery in his **studio** in the South of France.*

Picasso was now nearly 70 and one of the most famous people in the world. Crowds flocked to the Mediterranean coast at Antibes in the hope of catching a glimpse of him and his young family on the beach.

Picasso at Work

Françoise often watched Picasso as he painted. She later described how he would stand working at a **canvas** for up to four hours without getting tired. After a while, he would sit down in a chair and study what he had done. Then he would go back to the picture. He liked complete silence, and darkness everywhere except on the canvas.

AT WORK TILL THE END

All through his adult life, Picasso never stayed in one place for very long. Even in old age, he was restless and looking for fresh experiences. In 1953, Françoise left him and he soon found a new partner, Jacqueline Roque.

*A **portrait** of Jacqueline, painted in 1954*

The pair moved to a new home, a seaside villa near Cannes in the south of France. But soon they were off again, first to a romantic old mansion in a remote and beautiful valley and then to a home nearer the coast. Picasso and Jacqueline got married in 1961.

*Picasso made this painted **sculpture** of an owl from several different materials.*

He still worked amazingly hard. In the summer of 1968 he finished a series of 347 **engravings**. During 1969 he produced more than 200 paintings and drawings that went on display at nearby Avignon. It was only in 1973 that his incredible energy gave out. He died at the age of 91.

No End in Sight

*"One is never finished. There is never a moment when you can say: 'I have worked well, and tomorrow is Sunday.' As soon as you stop, it is only to start again. You put aside one **canvas** telling yourself you will not work on it any more. But you can never add THE END."*

Picasso

A Lasting Memory

Pablo Picasso was the most famous artist of the twentieth century. He was known throughout the world—even by people who knew nothing about art—simply by his name. Brilliant, daring, and dynamic, he seemed to be everyone's idea of a great painter.

His effect on the arts was enormous. Starting about 1901 he was at the center of a **revolution** in modern art that changed the way we look at life. He developed new ideas at great speed, and his pictures are filled with energy and dark emotions.

Picasso went on working hard until the very end of his long life.

A simple room at the Picasso Museum in Antibes, France

Picasso explored almost every branch of fine art. Besides being a painter, he was a **sculptor**, an engraver, an illustrator, a stage designer, and a potter. He produced a huge amount of work, much of which can be seen today in museums and **galleries** all over the world.

The Magic Name

Picasso is still by far the most popular of modern artists. Huge crowds flock to see his works. More than 100,000 visitors come each year to the Musée Picasso in Antibes, and similar numbers go to special Picasso museums in both Paris and Barcelona.

TIMELINE

1881 - October 25 – Pablo Ruiz y Picasso is born in Malaga, Spain

1891 – Family moves to northern Spain

1895 – Move to Barcelona. Picasso enters art school

1898 – Joins the artist community in Barcelona

1900 – First visit to Paris with Casamegas

1901 – Second trip to Paris. Suicide of Casamegas

1901-04 – The Blue Period

1904 – Meeting with Fernande Olivier

1904-07 – The Rose Period

1907 – Shocks the art world with *Les Demoiselles d'Avignon*

1912 – Begins making collages of pasted paper and other materials

1914-18 – World War I

1917 – Visit to Rome. Designs for the Russian Ballet

1918 – Marries Olga Koklova

1921 – Son Paulo born

1925 – Paints *Three Dancers*

1927 – Meets Marie-Thérèse Walter. Begins the *Vollard Suite*

1936 – Beginning of Spanish Civil War

1937 – Paints *Guernica*

1939-45 – World War II

1943 – Meets Françoise Gilot

1946 – Begins work in Grimaldi Palace, Antibes

1947 – Son Claude born

1949 – Designs dove peace symbol. Daughter Paloma born

1954 – Meets Jacqueline Roque

1961 – Marries Jacqueline and moves to country house near Cannes

1963 – Opening of the Picasso Museum in Barcelona

1966 – Major Picasso exhibition in Paris

1969 – Exhibition of a whole year's painting at Avignon

1973 - April 8 – Picasso dies at age 91

GLOSSARY

canvas heavy cloth material used as the base for an oil painting. Another name for a painting.

civil war fighting between citizens of the same country

Communist Party left-wing political party that believes in state control of property, production, and trade

construction piece of art made of different materials that is constructed, or put together, often using glue or nails

dealer person who makes money from buying and selling paintings

dictatorship rule by one person who has complete power

distorted strangely shaped

engraving picture printed from a block that is engraved, or cut, with a design

gallery place where works of art are shown in public

geometric using straight lines and simple shapes such as circles and squares

gigantic huge, enormous

harlequin traditional type of clown who wears a diamond-patterned costume and sometimes a mask

mythology having to do with legends or traditional stories

nationalist someone who has a huge pride in their country

paraffin waxy substance sometimes used in oil painting

portrait picture of a person or animal

prodigy child who shows exceptional talent

revolution complete change

sculptor person who carves shapes from wood, stone, or metal

sculpture shape carved from wood, stone, or metal

studio room where an artist works

study drawing or painting used as a sketch for a later painting

FURTHER READING AND INFORMATION

Kelly, True. *Pablo Picasso: Breaking all the Rules*. New York: Penguin Putnam, 2002.

Lowery, Linda. *Pablo Picasso*. Minneapolis: Lerner Publishing, 1999.

Mason, Antony. *In the Time of Picasso: The Foundations of Modern Art*. Brookfield, CT: Millbrook Press, 2002.

INDEX